ABORTION

DAVID ALTON with MARTIN FOLEY

ABORTION

Getting to the heart
of the matter

ST PAULS

Also in this series:
By David Alton with Martin Foley
Euthanasia – Getting to the heart of the matter

Also by David Alton:
Pilgrim Ways – Catholic Pilgrimage Sites in Britain and Ireland

ST PAULS Publishing
187 Battersea Bridge Road, London SW11 3AS, UK
www.stpauls.ie

Copyright © ST PAULS, 2005
ISBN 085439 691 8

Set by TuKan DTP, Fareham, UK
Printed by Progress Press Company Limited, Valletta, Malta

ST PAULS is an activity of the priests and brothers
of the Society of St Paul who proclaim the Gospel
through the media of social communication

Contents

Introduction   7

Joanna's Courage   20

Choices have consequences   39

Holly's tragedy   63

Roe vs. Wade – what happened next?   75

Conclusion   90

Appendix   96

Introduction

We live in a 'culture of death'. Around six hundred abortions take place every working day: six million since 1967. Since 1990 we have permitted the manipulation and destruction of more than one million human embryos in the name of medical science. Meanwhile, our courts sanction the withdrawal of artificially delivered food and fluids from patients who are not dying and parliamentarians seek to legalise euthanasia. Concern that this degradation of human dignity and disregard for the sanctity of human life continues unabated and virtually without demur prompted Martin Foley and me to write this book.

Those of us who continue to promote a counter-culture of life must struggle against an unsympathetic, if not hostile, legislature and judiciary and a media that all too often carelessly talks of rights – 'the right to choose', 'the right to die', without also stressing the importance of our corresponding duties. In such circumstances we need to understand the issues more clearly and become more vocal. We need to be pro-life in our deeds as well as our sentiments. We need to better understand how public policy is made and learn how to engage in a pluralist and democratic society. And we also need to look beyond our Parliament and courts to those who, by their daily lives and acts of witness, affirm a culture of life.

These individuals, by their campaigning work on behalf of the unborn and the terminally ill, by their work within the hospice movement, by the practical, financial and spiritual support they provide to expectant mothers and their families, and by their self-sacrifice, give us glimpses of what it truly means to uphold the sanctity of human life from conception until natural death. Through the cacophony of competing arguments the still small voice of personal sacrifice and example remains the most potent weapon for challenging and changing prevailing attitudes.

In a cynical world we need to be inspired and even the hardest of hearts must surely be moved by stories like that of Kelly Byrne, whose story I relate at the end of this book. Kelly gave her life for her unborn child. Her self-sacrifice was such a counter point to the self-centredness that characterises so much of our personal and communal behaviour.

It is, of course, true that in the very rare circumstances where two lives are in the balance an argument may be advanced for treatment to save one life while inevitably jeopardising another. This teenager's decision was to forego such a justification because of her overwhelming love for her child. How does her decision compare with those who take their child's life simply on 'social grounds' – the ground given in 98 per cent of the six million British abortions? Selflessness and selfishness stand here in sharp rebuke.

Kelly's poignant story is not unique. It echoes that of the famous Italian 'mother-martyr', Blessed Gianna Beretta Molla, who died aged forty, having demonstrated similar self-sacrifice and courage. Gianna combined a demanding pro- fessional career as a doctor in general practice with being a wife and mother to three children. Two months into her fourth pregnancy she was diagnosed with cancer of the womb and advised to have a hysterectomy to remove her womb.

This would have ended the life of her unborn child. As this was not the intentional outcome, only an inescapable side effect of the life-saving operation she so urgently needed, the hysterectomy would have been acceptable in terms of Catholic ethical teaching.

Despite this, Gianna chose to undergo limited surgery that she hoped would remove the cancer without harming her unborn child. The surgery was successful in terms of preserving the life of the unborn child but it failed to cure the cancer. Only one week after giving birth to a healthy baby girl, Gianna died on 28 April 1962.

Like Kelly, Gianna hoped that she would not die and leave her child motherless. However, both Kelly and Gianna clearly valued life to such an extent that they were prepared to give their children the opportunity to experience and enjoy life just as they had.

During Gianna's beatification ceremony in St Peter's Square, a young woman in her early forties knelt before Pope John Paul II for a special blessing. She was the daughter for whom Gianna had given her own life.

How can we think on this and not recall the countless unborn children who have been denied the opportunity that Gianna's daughter was granted? Our culture of death tells us that this is a sad fact of life – that regardless of the physical, emotional, and spiritual costs of abortion to women, the unborn and their families, we should not interfere in 'a woman's right to choose'. Pope

John Paul II has consistently spoken out about the corrosive effect of abortion on our society:

> The acceptance of abortion in the popular mind, in behaviour and even in law itself, is a telling sign of an extremely dangerous crisis of the moral sense, which is becoming more and more incapable of distinguishing between good and evil, even when the fundamental right to life is at stake. Given such a grave situation, we need now more than ever to have the courage to look the truth in the eye and to call things by their proper name, without yielding to convenient compromises or to the temptation of self-deception.[1]

It is so vital that courageous individuals continue to witness to a culture of life through their rejection of abortion, often at great personal and professional cost. We are not all called to acts of self-sacrifice like Kelly and Blessed Gianna but we are called, as Pope John Paul II says, to 'look the truth in the eye' and stand up and be counted. During years of campaigning on pro-life issues I have come across many people who have refused to allow themselves to be corrupted by the pro-abortion mentality of our age.

Barbara Janaway, for instance, was doing an 'ordinary' job – as a secretary in a medical practice. She was sacked by the Salford Health Authority for her refusal to type a letter of referral to a doctor so that a woman could obtain an abortion. 'I refused' she said, 'my conscientious objection was that I was setting the ball in motion. I would have been responsible.' An ordinary job, an extraordinary act, one which will have affected countless other people.

A friend of mine, whose story I recount later in this book, was told by staff in one of London's leading hospitals that his son would have spina bifida. Within forty-five minutes of the diagnosis he and his wife were offered an abortion. When he asked what experience the hospital had of postnatal treatment of spina bifida babies the doctor replied that even though the incidence had risen significantly 'only two are born here each year' (the rest are done away with). The hospital could offer no special expertise. Healers and defenders of life, or destroyers of life?

Samuel's father and mother knew that allowing him to be born would require great sacrifice by them – and it has. In today's climate their actions, too, were extraordinary – in the very best sense of that word – but a life was saved by their unwillingness to conform.

One of the great paradoxes of our time is the raft of new legislation to combat discrimination against the disabled set alongside the continued availability of abortion up to birth on the grounds of disability. In standing against this tide and by committing themselves to a life of undoubted inconvenience and sacrifice, Samuel's parents and others who allow their children to be born are surrendering something of themselves and witnessing against contemporary eugenics.

One of those mentioned here once said to me 'Anybody could do what I've done.' But generally, we don't. We conform and never even question what we are told by intellectual elites. We assume that laws and policies are enacted and implemented on the basis of mature reflection, wide-ranging ethical consideration, and a touchingly naïve belief that our leaders and decision makers will 'do the right thing.'

Let me give just an illustration of how these decisions are made in reality.

When in 1984 the Oxford philosopher, Baroness Mary Warnock, was appointed to chair the Committee that gave the go-ahead for human embryo experimentation, she told the BBC that she specifically vetoed the appointment of a particular member of the Committee on the grounds of his religious and moral beliefs. So much for democracy.

She graphically outlined the process of how the Committee was established:

> The potential Chairman is approached either by the Minister or by the Permanent Secretary or both. But, of course, one doesn't know how many other people have been approached.
>
> I sometimes get the feeling really that they sort of wade through dozens of names and then come up with someone who's a sucker and says yes. But, at any rate, after that, the thing is shrouded in mystery really.
>
> There exists what is generally known as the Central List. And the Central List is produced and combed for people who might have an interest in this kind of thing. I was then given a kind of draft list and asked whether there were any other people I thought would be obvious choices. Maybe people who were not yet among the great and the good. And I was with some difficulty allowed a power of veto.

She continued:

> There was one particular person who was supposed to be the Catholic and I said I would not have him. I just knew that I couldn't work with him. We went right up to the day

before publication with the civil servants saying, 'But there's nobody else in the world.'

So, in the end, the night before publication, I said, 'Well, will you please tell the Minister that it's a very, very bad way to embark on working on a committee when you know that there's somebody you're not going to find easy to work with.' The following morning two names were suggested. So I did win on that but it was very, very hard and it took a lot of persistence.

Persistence became precedence and the Government have enshrined the Warnock principle. Earlier this year they announced the new membership of the Human Genetics Commission. It's the same old faces and the same old opinions.

Among them is Professor John Harris – bioethicist and, surprise, surprise, member of the BMA Ethics Committee – who, in January 2004, expressed support for sex selection, with no personal objection in principle to methods used to achieve it, whether by sperm sorting, embryo selection or abortion.

When asked whether he would go one step further and endorse infanticide if a child of the undesired sex carrying a genetic disorder managed to remain undetected during pregnancy, Professor Harris responded, 'I don't think infanticide is always unjustifiable. I don't think it is plausible to think there is any moral change that occurs during the journey down the birth canal.'[2] He clarified that infanticide should not be used as a method of sex selection but that there are indeed circumstances when it would be justifiable to kill a child after it had been born. He declined to say up to what age he thought infanticide should be permitted.

> There is a very widespread and accepted practice of infanticide in most countries. We ought to be much more upfront about the ethics of all of this and ask ourselves the serious question: what do we really think is different between newborns and late foetuses?

> There is no obvious reason why one should think differently, from an ethical point of view, about a foetus when it's outside the womb rather than when it's inside the womb.[3]

Professor Harris believes that it is up to individual families to make a decision on the future of their child and he is not concerned that such a course of action could lead to infanticide for cosmetic reasons.

I don't believe there is any such thing as a slippery slope. I think that we are always on one. It is our responsibility not to avoid the moral choice.

We shouldn't make a bad decision now because we fear it will lead us to make another bad decision in the future. We should make a good decision now and have the courage to believe we will make a good decision in the future too.[4]

The Harris philosophy is that we do not matter morally simply by virtue of being members of the human race. Rather, 'persons' matter morally and a 'person' is an individual capable of valuing his/her own existence. As a result, embryos, foetuses, newborn babies, those in permanent vegetative state (PVS), patients with severe dementia and so on, are not 'persons' and cannot be wronged by being killed. On the other hand, some animals have greater ethical status than human beings as they have a greater capacity to value their own existence.

Thus embryo research, cloning, abortion and euthanasia are all perfectly acceptable according to Professor Harris. His is a crude philosophy that provides a 'one size fits all' solution to all of the major ethical issues of our day. It also makes him an ideal candidate for membership of prestigious committees. And, needless-to-say, he was one of the first to be invited to give evidence to the parliamentary Committee considering legalising euthanasia.

It says it all that you can argue for abortion, infanticide or euthanasia and the Government will appoint you as an ethical watchdog, but, whatever you do, don't call yourself a Christian or pro-life. If you do, there will be no room for you at their cosy table.

Another example was the parliamentary Committee that decided to permit so-called therapeutic cloning of human embryos (which involves their creation, manipulation, and then destruction). No one from the House of Lords who had spoken in the debate against cloning was appointed to the Committee and the one bishop who could be found in favour was appointed as its chairman. This was in contrast with the united view of nearly thirty theologians, Anglican, Catholic, Reformed and Orthodox, who gave evidence to the Committee re-stating the traditional belief in the sanctity of human life. One of the theologians was Rowan Williams, now Archbishop of Canterbury. Their evidence was not even cited in the Committee's report.

So, placing our reliance on this corrupted

process of public policy-making would be foolish indeed. Individually and collectively we need to be far more understanding of how we can best influence public policy and how we can best give practical help to those who are at risk. If this modest book is able to make a contribution to that process it will have achieved its purpose. In the Appendix you will find a list of useful contact details – individuals and organisations – that can help you promote a culture of life.

I reiterate my thanks to Martin Foley for all the effort he has put into bringing this project to birth and for his work as Clerk to the All Party Parliamentary Pro-Life Group. Let me also record my continuing gratitude to the group's Chairman, Jim Dobbin MP, to Mrs Phyllis Bowman of Right To Life, Professor Jack Scarisbrick of LIFE, Josephine Quintavalle of Comment On Reproductive Ethics, to Charlie Colchester of CARE and to all those who keep alive the cause of life.

NOTES

1 *Evangelium Vitae* (March 1995 para. 58); http://www.vatican.va/edocs/ENG0141/_INDEX.HTM
2 *Sunday Telegraph* (25 January 2004).
3 *Ibid.*
4 *Ibid.*

Joanna's courage

After years of hand wringing and indifference, 2004 was the year when abortion was thrust right back onto the political agenda. There were a multitude of reasons for this – not least the persistence of pro-life lobby groups, grisly newspaper stories detailing the horror of late term abortions and Professor Stuart Campbell's amazing 4D ultrasound pictures of the unborn child walking and smiling in the womb.

However, many feel that the real catalyst for the re-emergence of the abortion issue within public and political discourse was the courageous stand of a twenty-seven-year-old Anglican curate from Chester, the Rev Joanna Jepson.

Joanna was born with a cleft lip and palate. This is the same congenital abnormality which led an unnamed Herefordshire woman to abort her unborn child after the twenty-four-week legal limit in 2001.

According to the 1967 Abortion Act, a woman

is only allowed to do this if 'there is a substantial risk that if the child were born it would suffer from such physical or mental abnormalities as to be seriously handicapped.'[1]

When Joanna heard about this incident, she asked West Mercia police force to investigate the doctor who performed the abortion. After this request was refused, she applied for a judicial review of the decision in the High Court. A judge rejected the application, but the High Court subsequently granted permission for Joanna to challenge the police in court. The national and international media quickly picked up Joanna's case and the issue of abortion for disability or, as it should be called, eugenic abortion, became a hot topic of conversation in the UK and beyond.

Joanna's case arose because the Abortion Act 1967 (as amended) fails to provide a definition of the phrase 'seriously handicapped', leaving it to the discretion of parents and doctors. Some twenty-six abortions on unborn children with cleft palates have taken place since 1995, two of which were performed after twenty-four weeks. One in 700 children is born with a cleft lip and/ or palate.

Joanna's cleft lip and palate meant that her top jaw stuck out by about eight millimetres and her lower jaw hung down into her neck. She had to wait till her bones had stopped growing to have reconstructive surgery at seventeen. During her childhood, Joanna was forced to endure ridicule and abuse from her peers. She gained an important insight into the negative way in which society views people with disabilities.

Over two years, from 1991 to 1993, Joanna underwent three corrective operations to remove a strip of flesh from her upper jaw and to break her lower jaw, re-pinning it in the correct position. Her chin was then reconstructed from muscle. She was in intensive care for several days and the swelling took a year to go down. Her jaw was wired for seven weeks. After the surgery, which was offered as part of her orthodontic treatment, she had to carry a passport photograph around with her to prove to her peers that she was the same person.

In addition to her own experience, Joanna knew others who had cleft palates repaired and, like her, went through many operations in an attempt to correct their jaw defect.

She thought, 'If you play this argument through, the law is saying there are good reasons why I shouldn't be alive. And I look at my life and I think, "That's rubbish." Even if I hadn't had my surgery, even if I'd chosen to stay the way I looked before, that's no good reason for me not to be alive.'[2]

Another important factor in Joanna's decision to fight the scandal of eugenic abortion was her younger brother Alistair, who has Down's syndrome. The diagnosis of Down's in the unborn child is the most common reason given for late abortion.

> If you knew Alastair, if you knew my family, you wouldn't see anything as a disability. My brother is amazing. He loves taking photos. He takes these fantastic pictures of people that everyone else ignores – like the dustbin men, the postman or the workmen in the street. Somehow, these people are important to Alastair and I would never have seen that unless he had given me his take on the world. I want the opportunity for voices like Alastair's to be heard in society, not silenced before they have a chance to speak.[3]

Like countless others, Joanna felt that 'enough is enough'. Society tells us that every baby must be a perfect baby. Ultrasound scanning, which has done so much to capture the humanity of the unborn child, has also become the primary means through which physical abnormalities in the unborn child are detected. Pre-natal tests become 'search and destroy' missions with devastating results for the unborn child.

Joanna felt that the time had come to challenge the notion that success is all about being beautiful. 'Our society's values are becoming as vacuous as the reality TV contestants who embody them. I want the profile of this issue raised so that it is in the public consciousness that this is happening. This is where our enslavement to physical perfection and external beauty has got us.'[4]

Joanna's actions follow in a clear Judaeo-Christian tradition of respect for unborn life. Listing the habits of early Christians in the first few centuries after the birth of Christ, the writer of the *Epistle To Diognetus* stated quite emphatically: 'They do not destroy their offspring.' Literally translated, they do not 'cast away foetuses'.

At the heart of the gospel message is the idea captured in the Book of Genesis that all are made in the image of God – 'imago Dei', and therefore there must be a special regard and protection for the vulnerable. The unborn, I would argue, are some of the most defenceless people you can find, all the more so if they have a disability.

The central issue for the Christian is thus not the legal argument about whether a baby with a cleft palate is at risk of a serious disability. The question that many Christians are asking is why, in our age of relative enlightenment and equality, we have apparently enshrined in law far less protection for disabled children than for other children. What kind of message does it send to people with disabilities when they are singled out for abortion?

The courage displayed by Joanna in highlighting one particular abortion out of over 175,000 that are performed each year brought home the grim reality of abortion in the twenty-first century.

I have also been deeply moved by the experience of my close friend and colleague Jonathan Bartley whose wife gave birth a few years ago to a child, Samuel, with spina bifida. According to Jonathan, 'nothing prepares you for the cold reality of discovering that your own baby will be disabled, and the terrible difficulty of reconciling your well-meaning and deeply held principles with life choices.'[5]

Jonathan and his wife turned up at their local hospital for what they believed was a standard, twenty-one-week scan of their baby. Within an hour, they were sitting with half a dozen medical professionals as they explained that their child had a hole in the bottom of his spine, and that he would probably never walk.

Jonathan takes up the story:

Reeling from the shock, our first reaction was to ask what could be done. Surely, with all the advances in modern medicine, there was a procedure that could be performed? 'Of course, yes,' said the doctor. The terrible blackness that had enveloped us began to fade as we saw light breaking through. The doctor continued, 'You can have an abortion.' The medical team left the room, leaving us in terrible emotional confusion. Up to that point, we knew what our Christian convictions had been, but now we agonised about what our son's quality of life might be, how others would treat him, and indeed how we would cope. Theological reasoning did not seem applicable. Two years later, knowing Samuel as we now do, it seems inconceivable that we could have made any other decision. But we can also entirely understand how – in the context of fear, prevalent attitudes to disability, and the approach of the medical profession – parents in similar circumstances may make a different choice. The moment is fast approaching when we will have to explain to our son why, before he was born, amid all the uncertainty and emotional trauma of having a disabled child, the law was weighted against him rather than for his protection.[6]

The law has been weighted against unborn children with disabilities since the passage of the Abortion Act 1967 when Parliament decided that a pregnancy could be terminated by a registered medical practitioner if two registered medical practitioners are of the opinion, formed in good faith, that there is a substantial risk that if the child were born it would suffer from such physical or mental abnormalities as to be seriously handicapped. Subsequently, in 1990, Parliament decided to extend this provision authorising abortion up to, and including birth, on those who would otherwise be born with 'serious' disabilities. In almost all other instances the legal time limit for abortion is twenty-four weeks. At the time I described the provision as discriminatory and barbaric.

Proponents of abortion reassured Parliament and the public that abortion for disability would only be performed in extremely rare cases where the disability was so 'serious' as to leave the unborn child with little prospect of leading a 'meaningful life', whatever this may mean. What has happened in practice is that many conditions that are not 'serious' handicaps and were not intended to be covered by the 1990 amendment to section 1(1)(d) of the Abortion Act are now being used to justify abortions. We are witnessing the practice of eugenics, twenty-first-century style.

Abortion for cleft lip and cleft palate provides a graphic illustration of how section 1(1)(d) of the Abortion Act is being abused. Disability rights groups such as the Disability Rights Commission (DRC) and Disability Awareness in Action (DAA), although not coming at this issue from a pro-life standpoint, are extremely concerned about the application of section 1(1)(d) and the way it reinforces discrimination against people with disability. For example, in 2001 the DRC publicly stated that 'The section is offensive to many people; it reinforces negative stereotypes of disability and there is substantial support for the view that to permit terminations at any point during a pregnancy on the ground of risk of disability, while time limits apply to other grounds set out in the Abortion Act, is incompatible with valuing disability and non-disability equally.'[7]

I recognise the commitment of successive Governments to the eradication of discrimination against people with disability. The Disability Discrimination Act 1995 was a landmark piece of legislation and the present Government has signalled its intention to update this Act in order to tackle remaining areas of discrimination against people with disability when parliamentary time allows. This new legislation provides the Government with an ideal opportunity to address the concerns of the DRC and DAA and eradicate eugenic abortion. I won't be holding my breath.

In the years 1968 to 2001 inclusive, there were 4.56 million reported abortions performed on residents of England and Wales. Of these, 63,897, or 1.4 per cent, were performed under section 1(1)(d) of the Abortion Act – cases where there was a substantial risk that if the child were born it would suffer from such physical or mental abnormalities as to be seriously handicapped. The Government has acknowledged that the term 'seriously handicapped' has not been interpreted by any court decisions.[8] Joanna Jepson hopes to change this.

Since 1990, when the law was amended to allow post twenty-four-week gestation abortion for disability, the number of abortions performed under section 1(1)(d) as amended has increased substantially. In 1990, there were a total of 1,601 such abortions, twenty-one after twenty-four weeks gestation. In 1995 these figures had increased to 1,828, sixty-three after twenty-four weeks gestation. In 2002 there were a total of

1,863 abortions performed for disability, 110 after 24 weeks gestation.

A closer analysis of these disturbing figures proffers further cause for concern. The annual abortion statistics includes a table setting out the various conditions for which abortions under section 1(1)(d) have been performed. Looking at the 2002 Abortion Statistics I was shocked by the vague nature of the classification. For example, in 2002 eighty-three abortions were performed for 'other malformations of the brain', nineteen of these after twenty-four weeks gestation; four abortions were performed for 'eye, ear, face and neck' malformations; thirteen post twenty-four-week abortions were performed for malformations of 'the cardiovascular system'; and nineteen abortions were performed for malformations of 'the respiratory system', four after twenty-three weeks gestation. I could go on.

This vague classification is simply not good enough. When unborn lives are terminated for disability the least we should expect is a proper explanation of why.

The number of post-twenty-four-week gestation abortions for disability has risen exponentially since 1990. Since it is now generally acknowledged that after twenty-four weeks the unborn child is sentient and, if born prematurely, viable, one wonders whether the growing practice of post-twenty-four-week gestation abortion for disability is contrary to Articles 2 (right to life) and 3 (right not to be subject to inhuman and degrading treatment) of the European Convention on Human Rights which the Government has incorporated into UK law.

In 1996 the Royal College of Obstetricians and Gynaecologists (RCOG) published guidelines on the termination of pregnancy for foetal abnormality. According to the RCOG a person is only to be regarded as seriously handicapped if they need the support described in points 3 and 4 of the World Health Organisation's (WHO) scale of the severity of disability. Point 3 refers to 'assisted performance', the need for a helping hand. Point 4 refers to 'dependent performance', complete dependence on the presence of another person.

How can it be said that those unborn children with Down's Syndrome, of whom six were aborted at post-twenty-four weeks gestation in 2002, or those children with malformations of 'the eye, ear, face and neck', fall within the RCOG's and WHO's definition of 'seriously handicapped'? In the case of Re B (A minor) (Wardship: Medical Treatment) [1981] the courts held that it would be unlawful to withhold treatment to remove an intestinal blockage from a child with Down's as there was no evidence that it was in the child's best interests to die. If the courts regard the Down's child once born as not falling within the WHO's definition of disability, the same logic must apply to the Down's child in the womb.

According to the RCOG, one of the factors to be considered in assessing whether or not the unborn child would be seriously handicapped is the remediability of the condition. So how is it, as Joanna Jepson has shown, that over the past six years twenty-six babies have been aborted because of suspected cleft lip or cleft palate, one after twenty-four weeks gestation?

In their own guidelines, the RCOG states that when certifying that there is a 'substantial risk' of 'serious handicap' medical practitioners 'should bear in mind that the risk should also be likely to be considered substantial by informed persons with no personal involvement in the pregnancy and its outcome'. Note the use of the word 'informed'. Having spoken to medical practitioners I understand that current medical practice is such that obstetricians and gynaecologists do not refer to specialists in the condition that the unborn child suffers from. It is therefore doubtful whether they can obtain an accurate view as to whether or not the child has a serious handicap in any event. For example, when faced with a possible diagnosis of cleft palate, how many obstetricians and gynaecologists call in a specialist in cleft palate for their opinion as to its severity?

The terms 'cleft lip' and 'cleft palate' are used interchangeably, including in the official abortion statistics, but there is some difference. A cleft lip is a soft tissue developmental anomaly, which can exist without any underlying bony defects. As such, a cleft lip alone can usually be repaired successfully via plastic surgery at a very early stage, possibly requiring further plastic surgery at a later date. According to specialists in this field, whilst initially disfiguring, post-surgical cosmetic results are extremely good, often leaving nothing more than a surface scar which may be undetectable.

A cleft palate, on the other hand, is potentially a much more severe cosmetic and functional defect. It usually occurs in conjunction with a cleft lip and may be unilateral or bilateral. Management involves provision of prosthetic feeding plates as a neonate, significant bone grafting in childhood, extensive orthodontic management and replacement of missing teeth that are absent due to lack of supporting bone. Further plastic surgery may be required.

It is important to recognise that a cleft palate

is not a minor facial abnormality and can be severe. Nevertheless, cleft lip and cleft palate are not 'serious' handicaps for the purposes of section 1(1)(d) of the Abortion Act, satisfying neither the RCOG's nor the WHO's definition. The amendment to the Abortion Act in 1990 authorising abortion up to, and including birth, for disability, was not intended to lead to the rampant abuses that now occur.

In June 1990, when the House of Commons was considering extending the Abortion Act to allow abortion up to, and including birth, for disability, my colleagues and I received a legal opinion from Professor John Finnis and Professor John Keown, both of whom were at Oxford University at the time. Professors Finnis and Keown warned that the proposed legislation would lead to abortion until birth in a disturbingly wide range of cases and that 'some doctors will interpret the onerous conditions that apply to them as including a hare lip or a cleft palate'. Some MPs, including Lord Steel of Aikwood who, as the young Liberal MP David Steel promoted the original Abortion Act, ridiculed this interpretation. Frank Doran, the MP for Aberdeen Central, accused me and my colleagues of 'scaremongering' – an accusation levelled at me before when I have sought to draw attention within Parliament to the physical and psychological consequences of abortion – and Harriet Harman, the MP for Camberwell and Peckham, then a backbencher but now Solicitor General, suggested that Professors Keown and Finnis should be reported to the Law Society or to the Bar Council.[9]

In 1990 Frank Doran MP cited a paper from Professor Allan Templeton of the RCOG. Sadly this paper was not retained in either the Commons or Lords Library and I understand Professor Templeton no longer has a copy. In 1990 Mr Doran read from Professor Templeton's paper: 'It would be quite inappropriate for a variety of reasons to terminate pregnancies approaching the age of viability for reasons other than where the mother's life is at risk or there is a *lethal* (my emphasis) foetal abnormality'.[10]

How do Professor Templeton, Frank Doran and Harriet Harman reconcile such reference to 'lethal' abnormality with the twenty-six abortions for suspected cleft lip and palate in recent years, one after twenty-four weeks gestation, or the six post-twenty-four-week abortions in 2002 for Down's Syndrome? Having been proved utterly wrong an apology to Professors Finnis and Keown would also be in order.

Analysis of the Abortion Statistics since 1990

35

clearly demonstrates that section 1(1)(d) is being flouted on a regular basis and must be reviewed as a matter or urgency. When the lives of unborn children are being terminated in large, and ever increasing numbers, because of suspected cleft lip or cleft palate, or Down's syndrome, or ill defined malformations of 'the eye, ear, face and neck' or the 'respiratory system' it becomes nigh impossible to counter the charge that we are witnessing the practice of eugenics in twenty-first-century Britain.

Public opinion is increasingly concerned about the liberal interpretation of the Abortion Act, in particular of section 1(1)(d). Sadly one group that remains wholly ambivalent is the pro-abortion lobby. In an article *Termination Of Pregnancy For Reason of Foetal Disability: Are There Grounds For A Special Exemption in Law?*, Sally Sheldon and Stephen Wilkinson from Keele University argue that 'termination should be legally justified by the mere fact that a woman does not wish to continue with a pregnancy'.[11] This shrill pro-abortion rhetoric appears increasingly dated.

Ann Furedi, Chief Executive of the British Pregnancy Advisory Service, when asked about the application of section 1(1)(d) commented 'we have to trust the doctors involved'.[12] Her confidence in doctors is difficult to reconcile with the fact Furedi and BPAS have been consistently critical of doctors' involvement in abortion labelling them as 'judgmental, obstructive and unhelpful'.[13]

In the House of Commons a parliamentary motion calling upon the Government to review, as a matter of urgency, the liberal interpretation of section 1(1)(d) of the Abortion Act received broad cross-party support.[14] It was signed by members who would consider themselves pro-abortion and was even supported by the Vice-Chairman of the All-Party Pro-Choice Group, the MP for Richmond, Dr Jenny Tonge.

Disability rights groups such as the Disability Rights Commission and Disability Awareness in Action feel that a law that allows abortion up to birth for disability while allowing abortion up to twenty-four weeks gestation in all other cases entrenches the status of people with disability as second-class citizens.

The Rev Joanna Jepson has given us all a wake-up call. If, as a society, we are truly committed to equality and eradicating discrimination against people with disability then our first step must be to repeal a law – section 1(1)(d) of the Abortion Act 1967 (as amended) – that allows abortion solely on the grounds of disability.

Otherwise I fear that our commitment to universal human rights will be considered by subsequent generations to have been partial and meaningless.

NOTES

1 Section 1(1)(d) Abortion Act 1967 (as amended).

2 *Sunday Telegraph* (23 November 2003).

3 *Ibid.*

4 *Ibid.*

5 *The Guardian* (6 December 2003), 'Protecting the Disabled; Face to Faith', p.29.

6 *Ibid.*

7 http://news.bbc.co.uk/1/hi/health/1502827.stm

8 Hansard, House of Commons Written Answer (30 January 2004).

9 Hansard; 21 June 1990, Col. 1188; http://www.publications.parliament.uk/pa/cm198990/cmhansrd/1990-06-21/Debate-16.html

10 Hansard; 21 June 1990, Col. 1189; http://www.publications.parliament.uk/pa/cm198990/cmhansrd/1990-06-21/Debate-16.html

11 Sheldon, S. & Wilkinson, S. *Medical Law Review*, 'Termination of Pregnancy for Reasons of Foetal Disability: Are There Grounds for a Special Exception in Law?' (2001) Vol. 9, Issue 2 pp. 85-109.

12 http://news.bbc.co.uk/1/hi/health/3247916.stm

13 see the BPAS website: http://www.bpas.org.uk/page.asp?id=50&page=58&cont=62

14 http://edm.ais.co.uk/weblink/html/motion.html/ref=186

Choices have consequences

For as long as I can remember, the basis of the pro-abortion movement's argument for abortion has been that abortion is safe and legal. As the evidence detailing the physical and psychological consequences of abortion accumulates it is increasingly clear that while abortion may continue to be legal it is certainly not safe.

I recently met Margaret Cuthill, a Co-ordinator for British Victims of Abortion. She works with women who have been physically and psychologically damaged by abortion, helping them to come to terms with their abortion(s) and obtain physical, emotional and spiritual healing. Her own moving story is a damning indictment of the abortion industry in this country.

Margaret was involved in an affair with a married man at her place of work. She thought that this man was the love of her life. However, she fell pregnant and it soon became apparent to her that the father of her child was not going to risk his marriage and job by allowing details of his affair to be disclosed.

Whereas Margaret had initially experienced a sense of joy on discovering that she was pregnant, negative reasoning triggered a sense of denial and with it grew the panic experience so common in a crisis pregnancy. In that denial the baby became an 'it', a 'foetus', a 'product of conception', and a 'blob of cells'. It is so much easier to let go of a 'blob'. I have never yet met a mother-to-be who has told me that she was going to hospital to 'have a foetus'! Emasculation of language is a precondition when the life of the unborn is to be ended rather than birthed.

Margaret told me that 'with a determination based on rejection, panic and the necessity to survive' she found herself at the BPAS clinic in Liverpool situated in my then constituency, arranging the 'simple, straightforward operation' that many believe abortion to be.

No one at the clinic explained to Margaret the development of the baby. No one explained that there could be emotional or physical after-effects. According to Margaret, 'The choice was straightforward; they could solve the problem and no one would ever know… it was for the best…'

The abortion was performed on 4 October 1974. Margaret was in her mid-twenties and, on that day, Margaret believes that she began to live a lie. Her life would never be the same again.

During the weeks, months and years that followed, Margaret told herself that the fact that she became anorexic, was emotionally numb, felt empty inside and went from one destructive relationship to another had nothing to do with her abortion. She had a very successful career, and the abortion was no big deal. As far as Margaret was concerned it didn't really happen or it felt as if it had happened to someone else, not to her.

Eight years passed during which she was helped to submerge her real feelings by what she described to me as 'coping mechanisms'.

Then, Margaret's mother died unexpectedly. Her death came as a tremendous shock to Margaret, triggering a sense of loss which left her vulnerable in a way she did not expect. Margaret was thirty-seven years of age and literally on her own for the first time in her life.

At about this time Margaret was made redundant from British Steel with the option of being given a place in full-time education. She was accepted for a post-graduate course in Career Guidance.

Just before leaving British Steel Margaret had agreed to go out with one of the 'reps' she had met earlier in the year. They enjoyed each other's company but, being vulnerable because of her mother's death, Margaret thinks she saw more in the relationship than there was.

After a couple of dates, Margaret became pregnant. Two months after starting her new course, Margaret began experiencing the bodily changes which told her she was pregnant. Aged thirty-seven, Margaret experienced the same fear, panic and shame that she had experienced ten years ago.

The isolation and terror in knowing that she was repeating what she vowed would never happen again was 'awful… I felt that a woman like me deserved no better.' With the help of a friend Margaret arranged, once again, to go to Liverpool. Although ten years had passed since she last attended the BPAS clinic in Liverpool, Margaret told me that the counselling procedures had not changed one bit. The same automatic questions were put to Margaret:

'Did I think I could cope?' 'What were my circumstances?' 'Was I in a relationship or not?'

Margaret's only question was: 'It's just cells, isn't it? It's not a baby?' She was given this reply: 'No, it's not a baby.'

The abortion was performed and Margaret returned to college. Her workload was so heavy she did not go for the post-operative check until nearer to ten weeks after the operation rather than the usual six. She thought little of the fact that her periods had not returned or that she could not fasten her skirt.

Margaret experienced incredible shock when the examining doctor informed her that she was twenty-weeks pregnant. Margaret insisted that she had had the abortion and the doctor sent her for a scan to confirm the pregnancy.

The pregnancy was confirmed. According to Margaret, 'that afternoon at the hospital my denial in relation to what had happened in my first abortion was broken. When I was scanned what I saw was a baby ...**MY BABY** and I understood fully what I had done almost ten years before.'

Margaret was offered a further abortion which, having seen her baby on the ultrasound scan, she declined.

Later on, sitting at home, Margaret wanted to say sorry for her abortions but questioned whether she could be forgiven.

There was only one thing I could do and I began to pray and ask God for his help and forgiveness. There was no flash of lightning – instead came an inner peace which the Bible tells us passes all understanding. I did not know what the future held. But, deep inside I knew that I was not alone and I wasn't frightened of what the future might hold.

Four months later Margaret gave birth to a beautiful daughter, Pamela.

By now, Margaret was attending a local church. Although she shared the circumstances surrounding Pamela's birth, Margaret was too fearful of revealing the fact that Pamela had survived her second abortion, scared of rejection in the future.

At the time of my Private Member's Bill in 1987 when I sought to reduce the upper time limit on abortion to eighteen weeks, Margaret's church held a day of prayer on pro-life issues. A speaker from SPUC referred to post-abortion trauma and explained that a group from British Victims of Abortion (BVA) would be touring Scotland, where Margaret lived.

Margaret met this group from BVA and, with their help, started to come to terms with her abortions. For her, acknowledging her part in both abortions was a big step. But to know that she was not alone in her post-abortion trauma and that countless other women who were suffering physically and emotionally as a result of their abortions felt let down by the abortion industry gave much comfort.

For the first time I recognised that, although the responsibility for what had happened was mine, the pain I experienced, my anorexia, the loneliness and emptiness, were all valid and I had the right to grieve and deal with the loss of my child whom I named Jonathan. I was able to be the mother I had denied back in 1974.

Later, Margaret attended her first SPUC conference. One speaker explained that in the United States the incidence of abortion where one twin was destroyed and the other survived had increased. This, she was told, was more than likely what had happened in her case. Margaret told me that when she heard this her 'heart was broken'. She wanted to stand up and scream 'It's not true. It's not true.'

It took Margaret a further four years before she finally acknowledged this truth. By that time Margaret was convinced that she had overcome her post-abortion trauma. She had been working for over a year as Co-ordinator for British Victims of Abortion, a post to which she was appointed in October 1991.

Prior to this point, Margaret admits that she

had always evaded the matter by claiming that she could not be certain whether she had been expecting twins or whether Pamela had by a miracle been protected from the instruments used in a suction abortion. Now, however, Margaret recognised 'that the only way to heal is to face the truth head on, deal with the pain, confessing the part I had played in my abortion decision and allowing the Holy Spirit to cleanse and heal.'

Through prayer Margaret became convinced that she had lost another child, a boy, whom she named Christopher.

Margaret allowed me to recount her moving story to highlight the damage society is causing to women by promoting abortion as the simplest solution to the crisis pregnancy. She dedicates her story to her three children, Jonathan, Christopher and Pamela, and to the thousands of mothers, fathers, families and those in the wider society affected by an abortion experience that have been helped and supported by the BVA during the past seventeen years.

Margaret's story is just one out of thousands but it encapsulates the failure of the abortion industry to inform women that their choice to have an abortion carries with it physical and psychological consequences.

Despite the efforts of the pro-abortion

movement, post-abortion syndrome (PAS) is increasingly being recognised as a diagnosable clinical condition.

The psychological effects of abortion include post-traumatic stress disorder, sexual dysfunction, suicidal feelings, alcohol and drug abuse, eating disorders and child abuse.[1]

According to the charity LIFE, at least three English women embarked upon legal action because of the psychological damage which abortion did to them. The first woman, interviewed anonymously on BBC Radio 4's 'Today' programme on 13 June 2002, told how she had been so stricken with guilt and self-hatred – following the birth of a son nearly three years after an NHS abortion – that she effectively had a nervous breakdown.

A nurse, in her mid-twenties, she was given no warning about what abortion could do to her mental and physical health. There was no mention of psychological trauma, increased risk of breast cancer or any other damage. She wants to pursue the hospital not out of vengeance but for the benefit of other women.

The other two women tell similar stories. None of them had any pre-existing psychological problems. All of them insist that had they been told by the abortion industry of all the possible consequences they would never have consented to the operation. But women do not only suffer psychological sequelae: there are physical consequences too.

In recent years the safety of abortion and the failure of the abortion industry to properly inform women of the physical and psychological consequences of abortion has come under closer scrutiny as evidence has emerged identifying a possible link between induced abortion and breast cancer. Along with my colleagues in the All-Party Parliamentary Pro-life Group I have raised this issue in Parliament. Pro-abortionists also like to talk about 'choice' but, as the experience of women like Margaret Cuthill illustrates, such 'choice' is meaningless unless it is informed. We are forever told that we must have the 'right to choose'! What about the right to know?

Breast cancer is no trivial matter. It is the most common cancer in the UK and affects 41,000 women each year. It claimed 13,000 lives in 2001 making it the second most common cause of cancer death in women after lung cancer.

In Liverpool I chaired the successful appeal to build the NHS Linda McCartney Centre for women with breast cancer and am well aware of the suffering caused by this disease.

Substantial progress has already been made in

detection and improved treatment for breast cancer. However, one area that has been neglected is the association between induced abortion and breast cancer. I hope that the efforts of the pro-life community in highlighting the evidence linking induced abortion with breast cancer will further help reduce the incidence of breast cancer amongst women. This is not an exercise in scaremongering. I have never made any secret of my pro-life position on abortion. I would remain opposed to abortion even if it could be demonstrated that abortion has no adverse consequences for the women involved.

However, over some years now I have been studying the evidence linking induced abortion with breast cancer. I find this evidence quite compelling. Consequently, I am surprised and disappointed at the inadequate response from the Government, from the Royal College of Obstetricians and Gynaecologists (RCOG) and, regrettably, from cancer research charities.

Twenty-eight out of thirty-seven worldwide studies have independently linked induced abortion with breast cancer. Thirteen out of fifteen studies conducted on American women report increased risk. Seventeen studies are statistically significant, sixteen of which found increased risk.

The first epidemiological study was reported

in an English language journal in 1957. Researchers found a 160 per cent elevation in risk among women who had obtained abortions.

The first study to examine the abortion-breast cancer link among American women was published in 1981 and reported that abortion 'appears to cause a substantial increase in risk of subsequent breast cancer.' A 140 per cent risk elevation was reported.

In 1989 Howe et al. conducted a statistically significant study on American women in which medical records of abortion were used, not interviews after the fact. This study reported a 90 per cent increased risk of breast cancer among women in New York who had chosen abortion.[2]

Then, in 1996, Professor Joel Brind of Baruch College in New York and his colleagues at Pennsylvania State Medical College conducted a review and meta-analysis of the studies.[3] The Brind team, half of whom were abortion supporters, found an overall 30 per cent elevated risk among women choosing abortion after their first full term pregnancy and a 50 per cent elevated risk among women choosing abortion before their first full term pregnancy. I invited Professor Brind to Westminster where he detailed his findings. But his is not the only voice pointing to a link.

The wealth of evidence prompted Jane Orient, MD, a spokeswoman for the American Association of Physicians and Surgeons to declare: 'If you look at the number of studies that show a connection, they vastly outnumber the ones that don't, and the ones that don't have been criticised for serious methodological flaws... I think (doctors) should inform patients about this.'[4]

It is thought that there are two ways in which abortion may cause breast cancer.

Firstly, an induced abortion causes biological changes to occur in a woman's breasts which make her more susceptible to breast cancer.

When a woman becomes pregnant, her breasts enlarge. This occurs because a hormone called estradiol, a type of oestrogen, causes both the normal and pre-cancerous cells in the breast to multiply terrifically. This process is called 'proliferation'. By seven to eight weeks gestation, the estradiol level has increased by 500 per cent over what it was at the time of conception.

If the pregnancy is carried to term, a second process called 'differentiation' takes place. Differentiation is the shaping of cells into milk-producing tissue. It shuts off the cell multiplication process. This takes place at approximately thirty-two weeks gestation.

If the pregnancy is aborted, the woman is left

with more undifferentiated – and therefore cancer-vulnerable cells – than she had before she was pregnant. On the other hand, a full term pregnancy leaves a woman with more milk-producing differentiated cells, which means that she has fewer cancer-vulnerable cells in her breasts than she did before the pregnancy.

The second way in which it is claimed that induced abortion can cause breast cancer is through delayed first full term pregnancy.

Medical experts have recognised since 1970 that the earlier a woman has her first full term pregnancy (FFTP), the lower is her risk for breast cancer. A landmark Harvard study reported that for each one-year delay of a FFTP, risk is elevated 3.5 per cent.

The Lancet published a large meta-analysis on the benefits of breastfeeding and childbearing in which data were collected from forty-seven epidemiological studies in thirty countries. It was found that the relative risk of breast cancer declined 4.3 per cent for each twelve months of breastfeeding and 7 per cent for every birth. It was concluded that the incidence of breast cancer in developed nations could be reduced by more than half if women would bear more children and breastfeed for longer periods of time. Professor Valerie Beral of the Cancer Research

UK Epidemiology Unit in Oxford has acknowledged that 'the difference between breast cancer rates in developed and developing countries is largely due to the differences in childbearing and breastfeeding patterns.'[5]

One of the most common ways in which women delay their first full term pregnancy is by abortion.

When my colleagues and I have sought to draw attention to the evidence linking induced abortion with breast cancer, various objections have been raised.

First, it is said that there are major studies, based on medical records, not patient interviews, which show no difference in breast cancer rates between women that have had abortions and women that have not. The 1991 Lindefors-Harris et al study which appeared in the *American Journal of Epidemiology*[6] and the 1997 Melbye et al study from the *New England Journal of Medicine*[7] are often cited in this context.

Second, those who deny the possibility of a link between induced abortion and breast cancer argue that many of the studies reporting the link suffer from reporter or recall bias because women who have breast cancer more readily report abortions than women that do not have it. Alternatively, they claim 'editor' bias; papers that report the link between induced abortion and breast cancer are more likely to be accepted for publication than those which do not.

These objections fail to stand up to close scrutiny. The major studies cited as undermining any link are seriously flawed by misclassification and methodological errors. As for reporter or recall bias, this is pure hypothesis for which there is no evidence. The evidence for so-called 'editor' bias would appear to be only negative. Howe et al for instance were turned down by other journals before finding one ready to publish them.

In February 2000, the *New England Journal of Medicine*, possibly the world's most influential medical journal, acknowledged evidence of the link between induced abortion and breast cancer in an article written by researchers at the University of Pennsylvania School of Medicine.[8]

Dr Janet Daling and her colleagues at the Fred Hutchinson Cancer Research Centre in the United States were commissioned by the US National Cancer Institute to conduct a study to determine if induced abortion raises breast cancer risk.

Their study found that, 'among women who had been pregnant at least once, the risk of breast cancer in those who had experienced an induced abortion was 50 per cent higher than among other women.'

Daling identified three high risk groups and reported these findings:

- Women under the age of eighteen or over the age of twenty-nine who obtained induced abortions have more than a twofold increase in risk.

- Women with a family history of breast cancer who procured an abortion were found to have statistically significant risk increases of 80 per cent.

- Teenagers with a family history of the disease who procured abortions before the age of eighteen were found to have incalculably high risk. All twelve women in Daling's study with this background were diagnosed with breast cancer by the age of forty-five.[9]

The response from the RCOG and the Department of Health has been disappointing to say the least. In the RCOG's 2000 guidelines on the 'Care of Women Requesting Induced Abortion' they maintain that evidence of a link between induced abortion and breast cancer is 'inconclusive'.[10] Yet the RCOG has also acknowledged that the aforementioned meta-analysis produced by Professor Brind 'had no major methodological shortcomings and could not be disregarded.'[11]

It is impossible to reconcile the RCOG's two statements.

There are many factors contributing to the increased incidence of breast cancer. At regular intervals over recent years news stories have appeared citing research indicating that breast cancer is due to a decline in breast feeding, delayed childbearing, increased obesity and drinking, HRT and lack of regular exercise. Even deodorants are suspect. According to a report produced by Dr Phillippa Darbre, a cancer researcher at the University of Reading and published in the *Journal of Applied Toxicology*, deodorants contain a chemical which could be carcinogenic. Left breasts are more at risk because right-handed women, who are the majority, apply more deodorant to their left side!

All of this research is important because breast cancer is a multicausal disease: heredity, obesity, and lifestyles all play a part in its development. Women have a right to know about risk factors for breast cancer so as to enable them, if possible, to adjust their lifestyles accordingly. But why the silence on the most preventable risk factor for breast cancer – induced abortion? I am only too well aware that abortion remains a highly charged subject. One American doctor who has studied this issue closely recently declared under oath in a lawsuit; 'Over the past three or four years, I have spoken with many authorities and people in a position to be well informed. Some have been straightforward and said that they know it is a risk factor but felt it was "too political" to speak about.'[12]

In 2001 the Pension and Population Research Institute produced a study demonstrating that breast cancer rates had risen since the late 1980s in exactly the way in which, if more readily available abortion following the passing of the Abortion Act was a factor, one would have expected.[13] This was not proof of the link between induced abortion and breast cancer. It confirmed other findings. If it had shown no increase in breast cancer rates since 1967 it would have disproved the link.

However, the Pension and Population Research Institute is now predicting that by 2026 the annual figure for new cases of malignant breast cancer among women will have risen to 128,000. Breast cancer rates are growing faster among women over fifty. These are precisely the ones who have had more abortions, and more abortions of first pregnancies.

In the face of such mounting evidence it might be assumed that the Government and the medical establishment should sit up and take notice.

However, there is a catch. In March 2004 a paper in *The Lancet* entitled 'a collaborative reanalysis of data from fifty-three epidemiological studies, including 83,000 women with breast cancer from sixteen countries', by Valerie Beral et al. was published.[14] It has been widely touted as definitive proof that there is no link between induced abortion and the risk of subsequent breast cancer. In Beral's own words (as reported by the Associated Press): 'The totality of the worldwide epidemiological evidence indicates that pregnancies ended by induced abortion do not have adverse effects on women's subsequent risk of developing breast cancer'; and (as reported in the Atlanta Journal-Constitution), 'Scientifically, this really is a full analysis of the current data.'

However, according to Professor Joel Brind of the Breast Cancer Prevention Institute:

> In fact, the Beral study reanalysed the data only after a highly biased selection process which had many studies showing valid evidence of the ABC link inappropriately excluded, invalid studies whose flaws had been documented in the scientific literature inappropriately included, and valid studies whose data had been published simply not mentioned at all.[15]

This all points to a cover up. The abortion issue has always been highly politically charged and to acknowledge a link between induced abortion and the second most common cause of death in women would be a step too far for some.

However, I fear that if the Government fails to act and oblige the abortion industry to inform women about the evidence linking induced abortion and breast cancer, there will be class-action law suits similar to those we are witnessing against the tobacco industry. Years of denial and complacency could lead to billions of pounds in compensation.

In the US, two more States, Minnesota and Texas, have just passed informed consent statutes requiring abortion clinics to warn potential clients about the link between induced abortion and breast cancer.

The world's first known abortion-breast cancer settlement was reported in Australia in 2001. An Australian woman who had obtained an abortion sued her physician for medical malpractice. She claimed he failed to inform her of the research linking abortion with breast cancer and the possibility of emotional damage which she might suffer as a result of her abortion. Although she had not developed breast cancer she received a significant sum by way of settlement of her claim.

In 2003 in Philadelphia, a twenty-two-year-old woman who had an abortion aged seventeen became the first person in the United States to successfully settle a medical malpractice case based on a claim for the failure of her doctor and the abortion clinic to inform her of the increased risk of breast cancer due to abortion.

At the very least the Government should, as a matter of urgency, commission independent research into the possibility of a link between induced abortion and breast cancer.

It cannot be said that all women who have breast cancer have had abortions. Similarly, not all women who have had abortions will get breast cancer. Nevertheless, medical experts agree that women can significantly reduce their lifetime risk for breast cancer by: first, having an early first full-term pregnancy; second, bearing more children; and third, breast feeding for a longer lifetime duration.

Induced abortion causes women to change their childbearing patterns which, in turn, leads them to forego the protective effects of an early first full-term pregnancy, increased childbearing and breast feeding. Induced abortion is the most preventable risk factor for breast cancer. Young girls and women who abort before they've had a child – the majority of abortion patients in the UK – are at most danger.

For a long time, Margaret Cuthill was in denial about the psychological damage that abortion had done to her. British politicians and society are in a similar state of denial about the physical and psychological side effects of abortion, not least the link with breast cancer. If abortion can no longer be shown to be safe the question arises as to whether or not it should be legal in the first place.

In the UK, the Abortion Act gives women the 'Right to Choose' abortion over childbirth. Women also deserve the Right to Know exactly what this choice entails.

NOTES

1 For further information see the work of Dr David C. Reardon of the Elliot Institute in the United States: http://www.afterabortion.org/psychol.html

2 Howe et al. *International Journal of Epidemiology* (June 1989); 18(2):300-4.

3 Brind, et al. *Journal of Epidemiology Community Health* (1996); 50:481-96.

4 Dougherty, J., 'Can doctors be sued over abortion? Those who don't inform patients of breast cancer link could be targets', World Net Daily, www.worldnetdaily.com 27 March 2002.

5   *The Lancet* (20 July 2002), 360:187-95.

6   Lindefors-Harris BM, Eklund G, Adami HO, and Meirik O. Response bias in a case-control study: analysis utilizing comparitive data concerning legal abortions from two independent Swedish studies *American Journal of Epidemiology* (1991), 134(9):1003-1008.

7   Melbye et al. *New England Journal of Medicine* (9 January1997), 336(2):81-5.

8   Armstrong K., et al. 'Assessing the Risk of Breast Cancer', *New England Journal of Medicine* (2000); 342:564-71.

9   Daling et al. (1994) *J Natl Cancer Inst* 86:505-14.

10 http://www.rcog.org.uk/guidelines.asp?PageID=108&GuidelineID=31

11 'Evidence-based Guideline No. 7: The Care of Women Requesting Induced Abortion', RCOG Press, (2000), pp. 29-30.

12 Statement declared under oath by Angela Lanfranchi, M.D. in the lawsuit, Bernardo et al. v. Planned Parenthood, et al. Further information on: http://www.abortionbreastcancer.com/

13 Carroll, P. 'Abortion and other pregnancy related risk factors in female breast cancer'. London: Pension and Population Research Institute (2001).

14 *The Lancet* (2004), Collaborative Group of Hormonal Factors in Breast Cancer. Breast cancer and abortion: collaborative reanalysis of data from 53 epidemiological studies, including 83,000 women with breast cancer from 16 countries. 363:1007-16.

15 http://www.bcpinstitute.org/beralpaperanalysis.htm

Holly's tragedy

Holly Patterson was a seventeen-year-old Californian girl, who died in September 2003 after taking the abortion pill, often described as RU 486. Hers was a tragic and preventable death, one more casualty in the pro-abortion movement's unrelenting drive to make abortion more readily available.

Holly learned about her pregnancy in the second week of August 2003. She was so distraught over her unplanned pregnancy that, with the help of the twenty-four-year-old man by whom she fell pregnant, Holly sought help for depression from her family doctor on 10 September, the very day that she began the drug-induced abortion process. Her parents, Monty and Helen, were left completely in the dark.

Subsequently, Holly experienced severe cramping. She attended the emergency room at her local Valley Care Medical Centre, was given painkillers and then was sent home. That week-end Holly cried and complained to her parents of severe cramping and constipation. She allowed them to comfort her but could not tell them what she was really going through. On 17 September, Holly succumbed to septic shock and died while members of her family waited anxiously in the Critical Care Unit of their local hospital. The County Coroner determined that the abortion pill produced an incomplete abortion which caused an inflammation of the uterus resulting in a septic shock that ended in Holly's death. It was only after her death that Holly's parents became aware that their daughter had suffered a fatal reaction to a chemically-induced abortion.

In the light of Holly's death, the RU 486 Patient Health and Safety Protection Act has been introduced into the US Congress in an attempt to establish restrictions on the prescription of RU 486.

The tragic death of Holly Patterson after taking the abortion pill RU 486 is sadly not an isolated case. At least four women have died from RU 486 in North America and at least thirteen have required blood transfusions due to excessive blood loss.

In France, one woman has died after a chemically-induced abortion while others there suffered life-threatening heart attacks from the technique.

In January 2004 the UK Government disclosed that in recent years two suspected fatal reactions have been associated with chemically-induced abortion.[1] Despite repeated requests the Government has refused to disclose any further details about these two cases.

In the light of all this disturbing information all those concerned about women's health might have considered restricting the availability of chemically-induced abortion, at least until further safety tests have been carried out. This has not proved to be the case. Quite the reverse.

In June 2003 the House of Commons Health Select Committee published its report on Sexual Health.[2] At paragraph 33 of the report the Health Select Committee called for women to be allowed greater access 'to early medical abortion in a wider range of healthcare settings'. It was argued that this would help reduce the number of late abortions and would be 'a more cost-effective use of NHS resources'.

I have no doubt that in making their recommendation the Health Select Committee was heavily influenced by the lobbying of the pro-abortion movement, most notably by the British Pregnancy Advisory Service (BPAS). In

July 2003 an article appeared in *The Daily Telegraph* – 'DIY abortions at home should be given trial run.'[3] According to the article, the BPAS are pressing the Government to approve a pilot study of 500 home medical abortions using the abortion pill, RU 486. Then, in August 2004, another article appeared in *The Sunday Times:* 'British clinic plans do-it-yourself abortions from next month.'[4] The article detailed how the BPAS plan to allow women to take the abortion pill at home, without medical supervision.

Pro-abortion groups like the BPAS have always been unhappy with what they regard as the 'medicalisation' of abortion – the fact that two doctors must authorise each abortion, that abortions must be performed by a 'registered medical practitioner' (Abortion Act 1967 section 1(1)) and that abortions must be carried out in an NHS hospital or an approved independent sector place (section 1(3)). No doubt pro-abortions groups are also concerned at the steady stream of newspaper stories highlighting the distressing nature of late term abortion and the inherent humanity of the unborn child. For example, in June 2004 newspapers reported that the annual conference of the British Medical Association passed a motion requiring doctors to give the same level of neonatal care to babies that survive abortion as they do to premature babies.[5] There is also anecdotal evidence of increasing numbers of doctors who do not want to perform abortions, whether on grounds of conscience or because they regard abortion as a low-level technical procedure beneath their status as doctors.

Aware of growing repugnance towards abortion after the first trimester when the unborn child is more recognisably human, the pro-abortion lobby has chosen to focus its efforts on a liberalisation of the law on early chemically-induced abortion – that is, abortion up to about nine weeks gestation. They are also desperately fearful that as parameters are placed on absolute 'choice' the intellectual case for any kind of abortion at any stage becomes a more difficult argument to defend. For now, the pro-abortion lobby hopes to hold the line by exploiting people's lack of awareness about early foetal development and get away with the tired argument that what is being destroyed is 'just a bunch of cells'.

According to the 2002 Abortion Statistics, chemically-induced abortions accounted for 14 per cent of the overall number of abortions. Pro-abortion groups see increasing access to early medical abortion as a means of reducing the influence of the medical profession over the provision of abortion, as a means of allowing women greater responsibility for the decision to abort a pregnancy and as a means of allowing other health care professionals, particularly nurses and staff at family planning clinics, to play a greater role in the provision of abortion.

The Government's response to the Health Select Committee's report was not at all reassuring:

> We are actively considering what non-traditional settings may be suitable for medical termination... The Strategy Implementation Action Plan proposed that pilots be established to develop early abortion procedures, including medical abortion. Two pilot sites have now been identified the purpose of which is to enable the Government to define a 'class of place'. No 'class of place' will be approved unless the Government is content that a woman's safety is not at risk.[6]

Chemically-induced abortion or the RU 486 technique uses two powerful synthetic hormones with the generic names of mifepristone and misoprostol. It requires at least three trips to the abortion facility. In the first visit, the woman is given a physical examination, and if she has no obvious contra-indications ('red flags' such as smoking, asthma, high blood pressure, obesity, etc, that could make the drug deadly to her), she swallows the RU 486 pill, mifepristone. RU 486 blocks the action of progesterone, the natural hormone vital to maintaining the rich nutrient lining of the uterus. The developing baby starves as the nutrient lining disintegrates.

At a second visit thirty-six to forty-eight hours later, the woman is given a dose of artificial prostaglandins, usually misoprostol, which initiates uterine contractions and usually causes the embryonic baby to be expelled from the uterus. Most women abort during the four-hour waiting period at the clinic, but about 30 per cent abort later at home, work, or as many as five days later. A third visit about two weeks later determines whether the abortion has occurred or a surgical abortion is necessary to complete the procedure (surgical abortion is required in approximately 5 to 10 per cent of all cases).

It is this dose of misoprostol that the BPAS are pressing the Government to allow women to take at home, away from the clinic.

Notwithstanding the numerous deaths associated with chemically-induced abortion, the Government's failure to rule out the BPAS's demands for a liberalisation of the law on early medical abortion is additionally disturbing because there are serious, well-documented side effects associated with RU 486/prostaglandin abortions, including prolonged (up to forty-four days) and severe bleeding, nausea, vomiting, pain, and even death. In 5 to 8 per cent of cases RU 486 causes severe complications. Consider this 1990 statement from Edouard Sakiz, Chairman of Roussel-Uclaf, RU 486's French manufacturer:

> As Abortifacient procedures go RU 486 is not at all easy to use. In fact it is more complex to use than the technique of vacuum extraction… a woman who wants to end her pregnancy has to 'live' with her abortion for at least a week using this technique. It's an appalling psychological ordeal.

Danco, the drug's manufacturer, has reported at least 400 adverse events since RU 486 was first approved in the US by the Food and Drugs Administration (FDA). At a news conference on 17 May 2002, Dr Richard Hausknecht, medical director of Danco, the company which manufactures RU 486 for the American market, admitted, 'It (RU 486) is not safer than a surgical abortion.'

In April 2002 the FDA issued a warning to all healthcare professionals about the dangers of medical abortion, particularly if the pregnancy is ectopic.[7] Even China has banned all pharmaceutical sales of the drug citing safety concerns.

Long term effects of the drug have not yet been sufficiently studied, but there are reasons to believe that chemically-induced abortion could affect not only a woman's current pregnancy, but her future pregnancies as well, potentially inducing miscarriages or causing severe malformations in later children.

In the face of such overwhelming evidence about the damage that chemically-induced abortion can do to women's health, it is perverse for the Government to even consider allowing women to take the abortion pill at home. If abortion does have to take place, then surely all stages of the abortion should be conducted in an approved medical environment where medical assistance will be on hand immediately if required. Even then, fatalities can occur as the two recent deaths in the UK illustrate.

If mainly financial considerations influence Government to encourage women to complete medical abortions at home or at locations other than licensed medical establishments, no help will be available to the woman when her dead unborn child is expelled from her womb. What is she to do with her dead unborn child? What help will be on hand if she suffers heavy bleeding? Many women will worry about whether the procedure will work. (For up to one in ten women, it does not.) Many women will be inevitably plagued with questions about whether the unborn child is alive or dead, or suffering at any particular moment. When I have raised these issues directly with Government Ministers I have never received any plausible replies.

While there may be reasons for increasing the availability of, and access to, potentially life-saving or life-extending drugs, (such as in the case of AIDS treatments) no such reasons apply here. RU 486 is clearly intended only for non-therapeutic, elective abortions. There is no health crisis demanding this treatment. Women already have access to surgical abortion, which abortion proponents insist is already safe, effective, and inexpensive.

There is also an important legal argument at stake here. Under the Abortion Act 1967 (as amended), abortions must be performed by a 'registered medical practitioner' in an approved hospital or clinic. The case of Royal College of Nursing vs Department of Health (1981)[8] clarified the situation where surgical abortions are induced by nurses. The House of Lords held that even though the nurse may administer the abortion-inducing drug, the doctor has overall responsibility for the whole process and remains in charge throughout. The nurse's actions are done under his instruction in a 'ministerial capacity'.

I do not believe that the same conclusion can be reached when the woman can herself administer the second drug misoprostol at home. To allow women to take this second drug at home would necessitate a change in the Abortion Act itself. As the Prime Minister has previously stated that the Government has no intention of changing primary legislation in this area, it is difficult to see how the Government can satisfy the demands of the pro-abortion movement without acting illegally.

Rather than seeking to increase access to and availability of abortion – and calls to extend it to Northern Ireland, against the united wishes of the community who live there, is another example of this – we should be developing policies to reduce the appalling number of abortions that take place in Great Britain each year.

To accede to the abortion lobby's demands would be a dangerous and retrograde step. It would demonstrate that policy makers place pro-abortion ideology over and above women's health. We cannot afford to ignore the lessons from the deaths of women and young girls like Holly

Patterson. The Government must apply the cautionary principle. Before authorising pilot studies or general use of chemically-induced abortion there are myriad safety, legal and ethical issues to resolve. Failure to do so will result in women dying and eventually in class actions in the courts against the NHS.

NOTES

1   House of Commons Written Answer (12 January 2004); http://www.publications.parliament.uk/pa/cm200304/cmhansrd/vo040112/text/40112w31.htm#40112w31.html_sbhd5

2   Health Select Committee Third Report of Session 2002-03 on Sexual Health HC69-1; http://www.publications.parliament.uk/pa/cm200203/cmselect/cmhealth/69/6902.htm

3   Osborne, S., *The Daily Telegraph* (28 July 2003).

4   Templeton, S., *The Sunday Times* (8 August 2004, p.3).

5   *Liverpool Daily Post & Echo*, (2 July 2004, p.12) 'Babies Surviving Abortion Deserve Life'.

6   Government Response to the Health Select Committee Third Report of Session 2002-03 on Sexual Health HC69-1; http://www.dh.gov.uk/assetRoot/04/08/28/31/04082831.pdf

7   http://www.washingtonpost.com/ac2/wp-dyn?pagename=article&contentId=A5102-2002Apr17&notFound=true

8   1 All. E.R. 545.

Roe vs Wade – what happened next?

One of the main reasons why the abortion issue has been such a key political battleground in the United States over the past thirty years is because the United States abortion debate has seen some key players very publicly change their minds. By contrast, in the UK we have been time-locked in sterile debates about issues such as fox hunting.

The story of Dr Bernard Nathanson gives us an important insight into the pro-abortion movement.[1] In the 1960s and 70s their emotionally compelling slogan – 'my body, my choice' – comprised one of the most successful political marketing campaigns in history as abortion on demand became a reality in the United States, the United Kingdom and across the Western world. Since this time, these rallying cries have proved to be powerful rhetorical weapons in the fight against abortion.

'I remember laughing when we made those

slogans up', recalls Dr Bernard Nathanson, co-founder of the United States pro-abortion group the National Association for the Repeal of Abortion Laws (NARAL), reminiscing about the early days of the pro-abortion movement in the late 1960s and early 70s. NARAL has since renamed itself the National Abortion and Reproductive Rights Action League – far more politically correct.

'We were looking for some sexy, catchy slogans to capture public opinion. They were very cynical slogans then, just as all of these slogans today are very, very cynical.'

Dr Nathanson served as chairman of the executive committee of NARAL as well as its medical committee. He readily admits that he was one of the principal architects and strategists of the abortion movement in the United States.

Says Nathanson:

> In 1968 I met Lawrence Lader. Lader had just finished a book called *Abortion*, and in it had made the audacious demand that abortion should be legalised throughout the country. I had just finished a residency in obstetrics and gynaecology and was impressed with the number of women who were coming into our

clinics, wards and hospitals suffering from illegal, infected, botched abortions.

Lader and I were perfect for each other. We sat down and plotted out the organisation now known as NARAL. With Betty Friedan, we set up this organisation and began working on the strategy.

Nathanson and his allies quickly realised that they would need to persuade the media that establishing a right to abortion was liberal and progressive.

Knowing that if a true poll were taken, we would be soundly defeated, we simply fabricated the results of fictional polls. We announced to the media that we had taken polls and that 60 per cent of Americans were in favour of permissive abortion. This is the tactic of the self-fulfilling lie. Few people care to be in the minority.

Mirroring the approach of abortion advocates in the United Kingdom, Nathanson and his allies set about their task by fabricating the number of illegal abortions performed annually in the US. The actual figure was approaching 100,000, but the figure they gave to the media repeatedly was 1,000,000. Similarly, the number of women dying from illegal abortions was around 200-250 annually. The figure the pro-abortionists constantly gave to the media was 10,000.

This 'self-fulfilling lie' gradually seeped into the consciousness of ordinary Americans. Furthermore, the pro-abortion movement sought to convince the United States public that legalising abortion would not open the floodgates to abortion on demand and to abortion being used as a method of birth control.

In practice the annual number of abortions in the United States has increased by 1,500 per cent since legalisation. A similar phenomenon has been witnessed in the United Kingdom. In 2003 we had the highest number ever of recorded abortions, 181,600. In 1968, the first year after the passage of the Abortion Act 1967, there were a total of 23,641 abortions performed in England and Wales.

Within two years Dr Nathanson and his allies had succeeded in striking down a 140-year-old New York law outlawing abortion. New York immediately became the abortion capital for the eastern half of the United States. A brilliantly deceitful marketing campaign, bolstered by thoroughly fraudulent research, was paying dividends.

Nathanson himself established an abortion

clinic, the Centre for Reproductive and Sexual Health (CRASH), which operated in the east side of Manhattan. It had ten operating rooms, thirty-five doctors, eighty-five nurses. It operated seven days a week, from 8 am to midnight.

One hundred and twenty abortions were performed every day in that clinic. Within two years, 60,000 abortions had been performed. He personally performed 5,000 of these abortions. He now estimates that he has performed approximately 75,000 abortions in his life. With some justification he observes, 'those are pretty good credentials to speak on the subject of abortion.' It was film footage from this clinic that was the basis for the film *The Silent Scream* – that shows the unborn child trying to escape his instruments.

In time, Dr Nathanson came to realise that abortion is the unjust killing of a human baby. His powerful insider's account of the pro-abortion movement reveals the lies and exploitation of women that characterises it. I have little doubt that there are individuals in the United Kingdom who, like Dr Nathanson, used to work or perhaps still are working in the abortion industry and have a powerful story to tell. If we are to row back on over thirty-five years of legalised abortion in this country we need to hear from them.

However, the story of Dr Bernard Nathanson pales into insignificance beside the story of a Texan woman, Norma McCorvey.

Norma McCorvey was the pregnant woman known as 'Jane Roe' who made abortion legal in America in the historic Roe vs Wade Supreme Court case of 1973. She was the icon of the American abortion rights movement. In January of that year the Supreme Court ruled that the ban on abortion within the state of Texas infringed Norma's constitutional rights. As a result of this ruling abortion became legal in every state of the United States. For a time Norma became the heroine of the pro-abortion movement. Roe vs Wade was heralded as a fundamental breakthrough in human rights. In reality it has left a trail of bitterness and blood.

Throughout the world Norma's pseudonym is synonymous with the legalisation of abortion. Yet one aspect of the case which few people know is that having won her case she delivered her baby and gave her up for adoption: baby 'Roe' was never aborted. Although Norma went on to campaign for abortion and even worked in abortion centres, she later changed her mind, and in time also became a Catholic.

Now she is fighting in the US courts to get the Roe vs Wade ruling overturned.

When she came over to the United Kingdom in March 2004 at the invitation of the All-Party Parliamentary Pro-life Group (not the 'anti-abortion group' as the BBC have instructed their journalists to call us: we're not 'anti' anything we're positively pro-life, for the woman and her child), Norma spoke movingly and courageously of her shame at being 'Jane Roe'. She explained that in June 2003, along with hundreds of other women, she filed papers in the Federal District Court in Texas which she hopes will ultimately lead to the reversal of Roe vs Wade and give back to the individual US states the power to decide whether they want abortion or not.

Norma's moving story began in the early 1970s when, as a single woman, she became pregnant. Not wanting to keep her baby Norma travelled to an illegal abortion clinic in Dallas only to find it deserted. Everyone working at the clinic had been arrested the week before.

According to Norma, this illegal clinic was a pretty unsanitary place. Being put off by this, and believing that all the other illegal abortion clinics in Texas would be in a similar unsanitary condition, Norma changed her mind. She decided to have her baby and give the child up for adoption.

Having made her decision, Norma then met

what she describes as 'two ambitious lawyers with their own agenda.' They talked to Norma about a woman's 'right to choose' and how they wanted to see the ban on abortion within the United States declared unconstitutional. All they needed was a woman prepared to bring a test case against her state's refusal to allow her to have a legal abortion.

Convinced by their arguments, Norma agreed to become their 'guinea pig' and her legal case wound its way through the United States court system, beginning in her local District Court and ultimately reaching the Supreme Court. Norma describes her contact with her lawyers as 'sporadic'. Incredibly, she only found out that she had won in the Supreme Court by reading about it in the newspaper.

For several years, Norma was proud of what she and her lawyers had achieved. Roe vs Wade meant that women would no longer have to risk their lives in illegal, unhygienic back-street clinics. However, when a woman came up to her at an abortion rally in 1989 to thank Norma for her abortions, Norma sensed that something was wrong. 'She was using abortion as birth control. Call me naïve but I'd never thought of that before.'

Norma worked in four abortion clinics

between 1991 and 1995 but was fired from every one because she would sit and counsel the patients. When women presented for abortion she began urging them to 'search their heart and their soul: talk it over again with the child's father, with your parents, with your friends.' She would urge 'Why not carry the baby to full term and let it be adopted?' She was soon sacked. These clinics were often so filthy that they were no better than the back-street premises which legal abortion was supposed to replace. Norma also began to understand that few abortions had anything to do with hard cases.

When Norma spoke in Parliament she described how a woman in her second trimester began her abortion: 'She suddenly coughed and the baby was flushed out, still in the placenta sac. A new girl who was working with me lifted the sheet and said to me: "I thought you said they weren't babies." She was right. The foetus was very much a baby.'

Devastated by all of this, Norma became chronically depressed, began drinking heavily, and started to use drugs. She kept questioning what it was with which she had become synonymous.

There are now about 1.3 million abortions each year in the US, over 3,500 every working day: 150 every hour, one every twenty-four seconds. It is a fact that in the millennium year of 2000 more children died from abortion than the number of Americans who died in the Revolutionary War, the Civil War, World Wars I and II, and the wars in Korea, Vietnam, the Gulf and Iraq combined. More nascent American lives lost in one year than in all those conflicts put together.

The sheer scale of abortion is a key reason why Americans have become so passionate about this issue. As Norma McCorvey ruefully said at Westminster 'I don't feel heroic over a law that has killed millions of babies.'

Eventually Norma decided that she could not take any more of the abortion industry. In 1995 she literally moved next door from the abortion clinic at which she was working into the offices of the pro-life group Operation Rescue.

In 1998 she published her testimony *Won By Love* and established her own lay ministry, 'Roe No More'. Later in the year, she was received into the Catholic Church. She says that through her Christian faith she has been able 'to taste true love and the sense of forgiveness' that each of us needs. Roe No More says its mandate is 'to spread the truth and to know things as they are.' Her statement that 'I'm being true to myself and that is all that matters to me and God' is profoundly challenging to anyone who takes the trouble to listen to her.

For the past two years Norma has been helping to collect affidavits from post-abortive women for her lawsuit. Over 1,000 sworn affidavits have been collected to date. At Westminster she presented me with copies of some.

> The stories just break your heart. Most of them were either too young to understand or were forced into having an abortion by their parents or boyfriends. Some have suffered physical damage; one woman was left in pain for eight hours while the doctors argued over whether to kill both her twins at once or one today and the other tomorrow. She ended up sterile. All the women have suffered a lot of psychological and emotional damage.

The affidavits make for harrowing reading. They give the lie that choices carry no consequences. The law may say it's just 'my right to choose' but these accounts tell a very different story.

You cannot trivialise the taking of your own child's life. The developing life of a child cannot be reduced to yet another of life's choices. You may be able to scrape the baby out of a mother's womb, but never out of her heart.

What Norma McCorvey's story illustrates is that we don't need false moralising about all of this. Few of us are in a position to do that. But what we do need to do is to get real. Many of us have privately questioned the ethics of abortion but remained silent. We excuse our silence with phrases like 'I'm privately against but believe it's down to choice.' Imagine the response if I extended that argument to racism, homophobia, the sale of arms, exploitation of children or capital punishment. Privately against, but willing to sanction public laws would, at best, be greeted with howls of derision.

As Norma McCorvey observed: 'This has long ceased to be a feminist issue about a woman's right to choose.' Interestingly, Norma feels that the British are more liberal about abortion than the Americans. Norma McCorvey's reappraisal of the abortion issue is synonymous with the sea change that has taken place in the US. Although she says 'The British have never needed a Jane Roe. I heartily wish I had never been Jane Roe for my country', I suspect we now need a Norma McCorvey. We need someone who can blow the lid on the lies and vacuous compassion of the pro-abortion movement in our own country and radically challenge an approach that has inflicted such damage on so many women and their unborn children.

The decision of this one-time icon of the abortion rights movement to change her mind, and to spend her whole life working for the right to life, has acted as a catalyst in the US.

The number of abortions performed annually in the US has dropped to levels not seen since the late 1970s – and targeted and highly effective advertising in some States, pointing to the alternatives and offering practical help, has seen truly dramatic falls.

Norma knows better than anyone that she has taken on a powerful and well-organised industry. In 2003 alone the US abortion industry generated $400 million – and like its British counterpart it employs 'doctors' and 'nurses' who do nothing else. One doctor told a parliamentary committee chaired by Lord Rawlinson of Ewell QC that he had personally generated over £3 million in income from the abortions he had undertaken.[2]

In the same week that Norma came to London a survey of 5,000 British teenagers was published by *Bliss* magazine. It reported that two thirds of our teenage children believe that there are far too many abortions in Britain. In truth, when

2003 saw the highest ever number of recorded abortions in England and Wales at 181,600[3] and one in five pregnancies now ends in abortion, who could disagree?

Unlimited abortion has led to Britain's abandonment of a belief in the sanctity of human life with the result that one million human embryos have been destroyed or experimented upon in the past ten years. It has also led to the routine creation and destruction of human embryos for so-called 'therapeutic cloning'. We create life, only to plunder it for life-giving stem cells and then we destroy the donor. It's the ultimate in consumerism.

Perhaps Norma's courage in coming to Britain and telling her story might trigger a new debate about what it is we permit with barely a murmur of protest. Perhaps, as the *Bliss* magazine survey illustrates, the next generation of policy-makers will not be so weighed down with the ideological baggage of the present generation who came out of the political and social upheaval of the 1960s.

The United Kingdom equivalents of Bernard Nathanson and Norma McCorvey are out there. Like all of us, they just need to find their voice.

NOTES

1 Dr Nathanson's story is based on an article which appeared in the Pro-life infonet on 20 December 2002; http://priestsforlife.org/news/infonet/Infonet02-12-24.htm

2 Lord Rawlinson's Private Commission of Inquiry into the Operation and Consequences of the Abortion Act (1994), CARE, Romney Street, London.

3 Abortion Statistics, England and Wales (2003); http://www.publications.doh.gov.uk/public/sb0323.htm

Conclusion

When weighing up the controversial nature of the debate around abortion, bioethics, eugenics and euthanasia, it is tempting to duck for cover. Edmund Burke's dictum about the circumstances that are required to permit the triumph of evil springs to mind. Quietism can become a form of collaboration; after all, most of us would understandably prefer a quiet life.

At the very minimum we do at least need to take a healthy interest in the arguments that dominate these life and death issues. Often, in our own personal situations – for instance, the words we say to a friend or to a relative – we can deeply influence events.

Simply because we can't change everything – laws, policies, media attitude, whatever it might be – can never be an excuse for doing nothing. The Rabbi who famously said that the man who saves a single life saves the world, well understood the importance of personal actions, of how every individual can be an agent for change.

Sometimes this may involve paying a price. I was very moved by the story of Kelly Byrne.

Kelly came from Braintree in Essex. She had been suffering from leukaemia and made a desperate appeal to find a donor. She underwent a bone marrow transplant after a world-wide search found a suitable donor in America. After her treatment she was thought to be doing well, but developed pneumonia, and in her weakened state was unable to fight it off. She had been in a coma and died aged nineteen.

Kelly was pregnant when she found out that the leukaemia had returned. Kelly put off her radiotherapy and chemotherapy treatment in order to allow her son, Logan, to survive and be born.

Kelly's self-sacrifice and courage is an inspiration. So was the life of Ellen Wilkie.

Ellen became a good friend of mine. A disability rights campaigner, she was an indefatigable champion of the rights of the unborn. She struggled all her life with Duchenne muscular dystrophy, a very rare muscle-wasting disease. Most of us could not hope to pack into our entire lives what Ellen achieved in her short thirty-one years; she got an honours degree in Classics from Bristol University, she was a published poet, prison worker, author, actress, radio and television presenter, journalist and musician – the list goes on.

When asked to address a school assembly about her achievements she said, 'It would make a boring assembly. Anybody could do what I've done.' Whether anyone could in fact do what she did is debatable. The point is that anyone might do what she did. Her life and approach to life should be an inspiration to us all. Ellen once said to me: 'I did not see how anyone could be part of the disability movement and advocate abortion on the grounds of disability.'

Anita Anderson was one of my constituents in Liverpool. In 1993 she became pregnant and was told that a scan had revealed a chink in her unborn baby's leg. She declined the abortion which she was offered. After her next scan she was told that the child would suffer from dwarfism. She again declined an abortion. On a third occasion she was told that the baby was growing again but would be multiply handi-capped. Following her third refusal, a social worker arrived at her mother's home and told her mother that a hospital bed had been booked for an abortion on the following Monday. What presumptuous arrogance, and what extraordinary pressure! The baby's father, Terry Anderson, told me that although he was not a regular church-goer, he was certain that abortion was wrong. Spiritually they needed great strength, and Terry privately visited a local church and lit devotional candles and prayed. Their faith and strength were rewarded by the birth of a perfectly healthy little girl; but as Mr Anderson remarked: 'What should have been the happiest time of our lives was turned into a nightmare.' Anita Anderson adds:

> They treated me totally the wrong way. They didn't think about my feelings. They made me feel as if I was carrying a guinea pig and as if they just wanted me to have an abortion so they could carry it away. I was crying all the time. One night I woke up and thought I was going to have a nervous breakdown. It was just disturbing.

I raised this case directly at a meeting with the then Health Secretary. He agreed that tests should not lead to directional counselling. In reality, diagnostic tests are routinely treated as the first part of a search-and-destroy mission, and intolerable pressure is placed on parents to follow the logic of the tests. Cures are not available, but abortion is. Far from being reliable, the tests lead to perfectly healthy unborn babies being aborted, and to the subsequent trauma of angry parents suing health authorities for negligence and incompetence. It also led to a British mother saying she would sue the doctors who failed to test successfully for the spina bifida which affects her son.

I do not have an idealised or romanticised view of disability. But I do have a trenchant view about the dignity and rights of disabled people and the duty of society to speak up for them and to protect them. I feel the same way about the terminally ill and about the unborn. All have a right to life upon recognition of which, as Pope John Paul II declares at the beginning of his inspirational encyclical *Evangelium Vitae* (the Gospel of Life), 'every human community and the political community itself are founded.'[1]

In the Roman Empire unwanted babies were 'exposed' and left to die. Our degraded view of the intrinsic value of every person is little better. These life issues go to the very heart of what it is to be human. In many respects they are the defining issues of our age.

In a twelve-month period that has taken me to countries whose people have been plagued by genocide and atrocities – Burma, Sudan, Congo and Rwanda; to the favellas of Brazil – where between four and five children and adolescents